Great Railway Paintings
Inspired by the Seaside

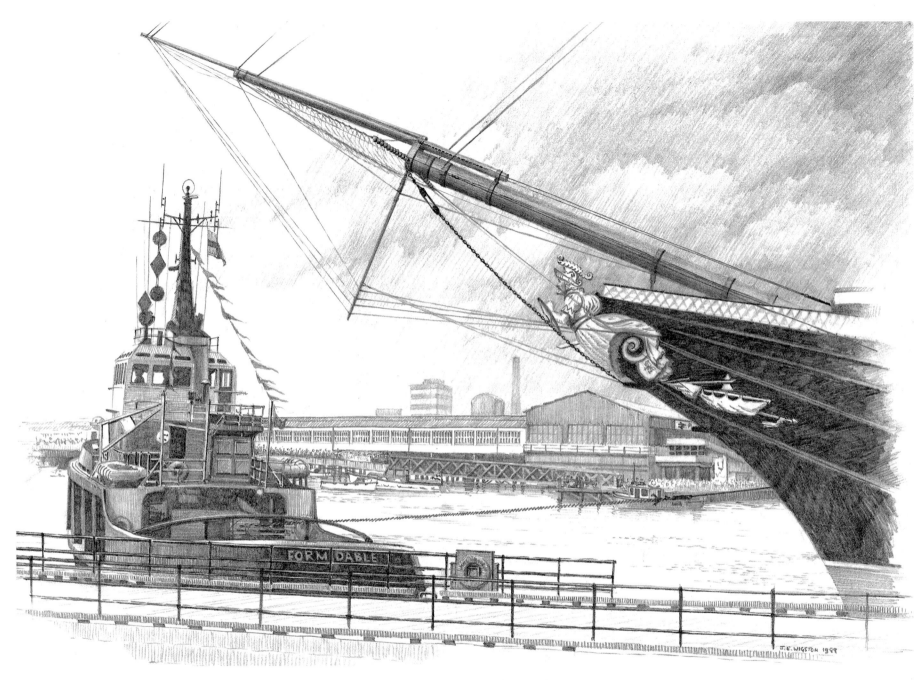

A Warrior's Return (see p. 78)
John E. Wigston, GRA

Great Railway Paintings
Inspired by the Seaside

THE GUILD OF RAILWAY ARTISTS

D&C
David and Charles

To Frank and Steve

Contents page: **Royal Albert Bridge, Saltash** (see p. 78)
G. Peter M. Green, GRA

Acknowledgements page: **Norfolk Ferry Departure** (see p.78)
Rob Milliken, GRA

A DAVID & CHARLES BOOK
David & Charles is a subsidiary of F+W (UK) Ltd.,
an F+W Publications Inc. company

First published in the UK in 1990 as *To the Seaside*
First paperback edition 2005

A catalogue record for this book is available from the British Library.

ISBN 0 7153 2211 7

Printed in Singapore by KHL Printing Co Pte Ltd
for David & Charles
Brunel House   Newton Abbot   Devon

Visit our website at www.davidandcharles.co.uk

David & Charles books are available from all good bookshops; alternatively you can contact our
Orderline on (0)1626 334555 or write to us at FREEPOST EX2 110, David & Charles Direct,
Newton Abbot, TQ12 4ZZ (no stamp required UK mainland).

CONTENTS

ACKNOWLEDGEMENTS

The Guild is indebted to its member artists, both those included in this collection of works of art and those who are not, whose time and effort in producing paintings and drawings that were ultimately not selected is greatly appreciated. Without the sterling efforts of all concerned, *To the Seaside* would not have become a reality.

The Guild expresses its thanks to the publishers for their invaluable help and assistance and to Richard Erven, who has once again 'believed in us'.

The Guild thanks most sincerely Peter Clayton for his most eloquent illumination of the subject.

The Guild also expresses its thanks to Ellis James-Robertson for acting as the Art Co-ordinator of the project (a most thankless task!) and to the members of the Guild Selection Panel for what became one of the most onerous and daunting tasks they have perhaps undertaken.

The Guild would also like to thank sincerely the following: John Wright Photography of Warwick for the photography of the colour plates.
The art galleries who have allowed the Guild to take *To the Seaside* to the seaside!: Torre Abbey, Torquay; The Woodspring Museum, Weston Super Mare; The Art Gallery and Museum, Hastings; The Welholme Galleries, Great Grimsby and The Europa Gallery, Sutton, Surrey.

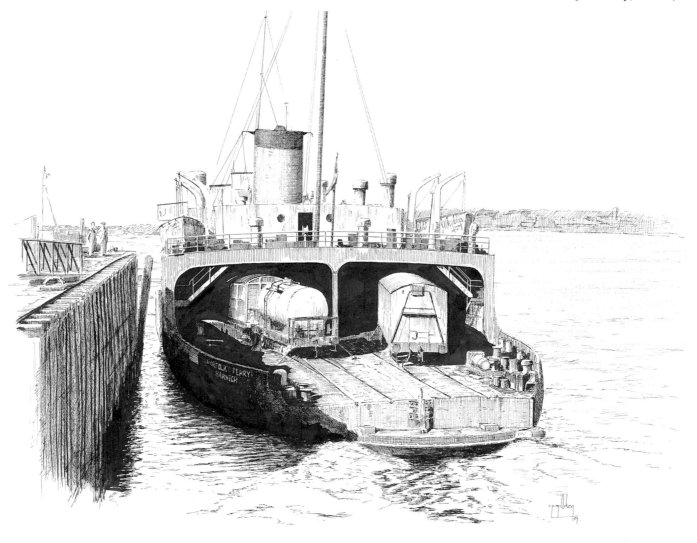

FOREWORD

Terence Cuneo, OBE, RGI, FGRA

Getting to school from my home in St Ives, Cornwall, entailed a hefty journey. For these occasions I would travel on the Cornish Riviera Express. One day I found myself having to sit for lunch in the dining car with three complete strangers. The passenger next to me was an elderly lady of enormous dignity. I was in the act of nervously helping myself to peas from the dish held by the attendant when the coach, clattering over points, shook violently and I deposited the entire load in the lady's lap! Puce with embarrassment I muttered an apology and attempted to shovel the things back onto my plate. In rigid silence, the woman surveyed me as if I had turned into some loathsome slug that had reared up from her salad. My efforts to retrieve the peas proved to be far more successful in mashing them into her Harris tweed than in restoring them to my plate. This ordeal, coming as it did at an impressionable age, put me off dining cars for terms to come!

Then there was the St Ives Lifeboat. The launching of this was, a strangely ludicrous affair and often hilariously funny. The boathouse was situated at one extremity of the harbour; the slipway, for some obscure reason, was at the other, opposite the Sloop Inn. On the occasions when the maroon went off, a ponderous ritual would creak into action. Doors were flung open and the lifeboat emerged, hauled by the gallant crew, and protesting and clanking on its caterpillar wheels. Immediately the boat was clear of its house, it had to be turned sharp left to avoid the harbour wall, this maneouvre being carried out in a series of thrusts, to and fro, to yells of 'Hold hard, there!', 'To you, Charlie', 'Back her up, m'dear', each utterance punctuated by blasts from the boatswain's whistle. Once on the straight, things would look better, until everything came to a sudden halt as an error of steering brought the boat's bows dangerously near an overhanging building. More whistling, caterpillars clanking back and forth, then off again, a muddled cavalcade of crew, lifeboat and townsfolk lurching towards the sea. At the Sloop, a brisk right turn and a heartening acceleration as the boat, cheered by a delighted crowd, clattered bravely down the slipway. If, however (as nearly always seemed to be the case), the tide was out, a further series of frantic maneouvres might ensue so as to avoid lobster pots, boats, anchor chains and other obstacles calculated to thwart the 'mission of mercy'. By the time the sea was finally reached there was just a sporting chance that one or two survivors had swum ashore and were lending a hand with the launching!

Hardly 'seaside' tales you might think, but nevertheless connected with so many memories of my seaside holidays. Returning in the train from school, for instance, I would stand at the carriage window, eagerly waiting for the train to emerge from a certain tunnel west of Dawlish and into view of the famous 'old man' rock, which, for me, stood as the emblem of sea and freedom. My rock – the 'hols' had indeed *started*!

Those summer holidays were never to be forgotten. Swimming with my friends on perfect sandy beaches, with often not a soul to be seen; climbing up perilous rocks, exploring mysterious caves and generally having the time of our lives; there never seemed to be crowds anywhere in Cornwall in those days, and the sense of freedom was intoxicating.

Looking through the pages of this delightful book brings back many memories. The illustrations are both graphic and in some cases charmingly nostalgic, and I have no doubt that *To the Seaside* will become a collector's piece and a must for any railway enthusiast. Although my own seaside holidays are now mostly things of the past, the seaside is forever. The fascination of being there beside it, to smell salt-laden air, hear the thunder of breakers unfolding along a beach, race barefooted along the sand and plunge into buoyant water – these magical elements will have the crowds surging to our coastlines till the end of time.

I wish this excellent book every success and am delighted to see that the very first painting, by Lawrence Hammonds, depicts the dear little branch line station of St Ives, a station so intimately connected with all my own treasured memories of seaside holidays.

Terence Cuneo

INTRODUCTION

Railways have been valid subject matter for the artist since the birth of this form of transportation. Frith, Monet and Turner made their indelible mark upon the world of art with their portrayals of matters railway, either as technical records or as artistic impressions. These early classical excursions into the subject have been continued by artists in every succeeding generation.

In 1979 artists, for the first time, had the opportunity of joining an association bringing them together as an art guild. From some sixteen founder members, the Guild of Railway Artists has grown in membership and stature to well over a hundred artists in its first decade. Its members include both professional and semi-professional artists. Portrayals are executed by the members in most of the major art media in use today – oils, acrylics, watercolour etc – and the subject matter covers the whole breadth of the railway scene. The Guild has exhibited its members' works of art frequently since 1979 at art galleries and museums throughout the country.

The Guild's first entrance into the world of publishing came in 1985 with the release of its very successful thematic collection, 'The Great Western Collection'. An exhibition of the works of art contained within the book was toured on the British Rail Western Region GWR150 Exhibition Train, and taken to the 3rd International Model Railway Festival held in Frankfurt, West Germany.

By 1987 the Guild's Management Committee were discussing in depth the possibilities of a new art collection suitable for both publication and subsequent exhibition. Many subjects were suggested; however, we were seeking a theme that would give both the broadest possible breadth of subject matter for portrayal and, hopefully, a maximum impact upon the reader or visitor to the exhibitions. 'To the Seaside' became the chosen theme and in June of 1988 we gave the Members of the Guild notice of the project. That notice is reproduced here, for we believe it says everything about this collection of works of art that could be said.

How do we see 'To the Seaside' – well what are your early memories! – your annual holiday with Mum and Dad by train to that 'exotic resort'! – perhaps in the South West or the North East! – with memories of sunny days, buckets and spades, the ever-changing view from the carriage window! that first glimpse of the sea! the sad return home knowing that holidays were over for another year!!! – but that is not all of what 'To the Seaside' is about – most railways ran to the sea – with passengers, goods, freight – all gauges of railway can be found running to the sea – railway-owned aeroplanes flew to the seaside, railway company boats and other vessels sailed to and from the multitude of docks around our coast, and buses plied to and from the stations to either bring us nearer the sea or take us inland to villages and hamlets away from the coast. Expresses from the London termini bounded relentlessly to their chosen resorts. The resorts even built their own miniature railways for the amusement of its visitors and some even had 'Trams!' – even in the modern world our resorts still abound with 'railway' – the funfairs are, if you look, very much reliant upon the rail be it miniature railway, monorail etc. 'People' went, and still go, to the seaside – and 'other people' help those 'people' go to the seaside!!

Since railways began they have been inextricably linked with the sea. We feel after some thought that there is such a wealth of possible depictions that could be done (with a little original thought!), that this Collection must artistically be far beyond even the heights we have achieved before – We therefore hand it over to you our Members – How do you see 'To the Seaside' – all we ask is that each depiction must have some link with the title.

We commend this book to you the reader and hope that you gain as much enjoyment from it as we have whilst assembling this collection of works of art by some of the most talented artists in the country.

Frank Hodges
HONORARY ADMINISTRATOR
GUILD OF RAILWAY ARTISTS

Stephen Johnson
HONORARY CO-ORDINATOR
GUILD OF RAILWAY ARTISTS

TO THE SEASIDE

For a so-called Island Race, it was a long time before the bulk of ordinary Britons – except those who lived by it already – managed to get even a look at the water which surrounded them. The upper crust, who could afford such luxuries as travel, hypochondria and – thanks to their over-indulgent lifestyle – genuine illness, had started to make regular visits to certain favoured coastal towns and villages during the eighteenth century. But, no matter what ancillary pleasures were provided, the fundamental purpose of these trips was medicinal. As early as 1660 a Dr Wittie in Scarborough was proclaiming in print the curative properties of sea water, advising his readers not only to bathe in it but to drink the stuff as well.

The physician who contributed most to this maritime branch of medicine was Dr Richard Russell. In 1750 he published a book on the benefits conferred by immersing the body in sea water, and, three years later, as if to demonstrate the courage of his convictions, he moved from Lewes, a little way inland, to the nearby village of Brighthelmstone. The nineteenth and twentieth centuries came to know it, more simply, as Brighton.

At about the same time that Dr Russell made his move to the seaside (although that word did not come into general use until later), a Quaker in Margate named Benjamin Beale invented the bathing machine. This was essentially a horse-drawn van in which the intending bather was trundled out to a suitable depth, at which point he or she would descend into the water protected from public gaze by a large awning.

The well-to-do went through this elaborate routine not because they enjoyed it (how could they, since it often took place as early as 6am and as late as November?) but because they had been conned into believing that it 'Did Them Good'. When the lower orders finally broke through to the beaches – a kind of invasion in reverse – they neither knew nor cared what some fashionable doctor had once ordered; what they wanted was an escape from the daily grind of life in the back streets of unlovely industrial towns or respectable but drab suburbs.

Some genius invented the knotted handkerchief – the poor man's solar topee. In due course trousers were rolled up to the knee and skirts tucked into knickers to make possible the British nautical compromise of paddling. Piers waded out into the water further than any mere paddler could, providing a narrow extension of the land dedicated entirely to pleasure. The pier at Southend was so long that eventually a tramway ran from end to end; but then, Southend was a special case, its 'beach' at low tide being in reality a vast stretch of estuarine mud which provided generations of comedians with jokes. It was Gillie Potter, I think, who said he once went to Southend 'to watch them ploughing'. Fanciful bandstands in overwrought iron sprang up on promenades so that, as the song put it, while the brass band played 'tiddly om-pom-pom' in the dry, the listeners, if any, got wet.

Somewhere along the way came the invention of lettered rock, a confection only slightly harder than the geological kind, and with the added distinction of being in the form of sticks with the name of the resort – for example ƎTAƆЯAM – cunningly arranged to run right through the middle. Over the years small children must have consumed miles of rock, steadily gnawing, sucking and crunching their way towards certain dental decay. These same small children were quick to recognise the civil

The Devonian (see p. 78)
Philip D. Hawkins, GRA

engineering possibilities inherent in sand, which meant that the bucket and spade became items of equipment that no family visiting the seaside could afford to be without.

The fact that during the second half of the nineteenth century and the first half of the twentieth, steadily increasing numbers of such families – ordinary, humble, struggling-to-make-ends-meet families – could get to the seaside at all was the result of one invention to which all others were subsidiary: the railway.

In American folklore the railroad became the symbol of genuine escape, of moving on to a new life or getting away as far as possible from an old one. The sheer size of the trains, the distances they covered, and the often rugged nature of the terrain they ran through, imbued them with a romanticism that was simply not possible in a land where the sea was never more than 80 miles away. So in the British Isles the railway acquired a more cosy significance and established a relationship based on affection rather than awe. Maybe it did rumble and clank throughout the night, carrying what the Americans called freight and the British called goods, and maybe it did convey thousands upon thousands of breadwinners to and from their mundane work every day. What really mattered was that for those who could get away at all, either for a holiday or just for the day, it was the railway that took them. It was difficult, therefore, to look upon such a benefactor as anything but a good friend.

Paternalistic employers saw the railway in that light too. In a Liverpool bookshop a few years ago I came across a facsimile reprint of a ninety-six page booklet which a huge Burton-on-Trent brewery had issued free to its employees on the occasion of the firm's outing to Liverpool and New Brighton in the summer of 1904. It is an amazing document. For a start it

Edwardian Heatwave (see p. 78)
Roy Putt

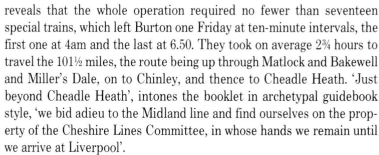

reveals that the whole operation required no fewer than seventeen special trains, which left Burton one Friday at ten-minute intervals, the first one at 4am and the last at 6.50. They took on average 2¾ hours to travel the 101½ miles, the route being up through Matlock and Bakewell and Miller's Dale, on to Chinley, and thence to Cheadle Heath. 'Just beyond Cheadle Heath', intones the booklet in archetypal guidebook style, 'we bid adieu to the Midland line and find ourselves on the property of the Cheshire Lines Committee, in whose hands we remain until we arrive at Liverpool'.

The booklet also points out, however, that Midland engines would work the trains the whole way and informs the brewery workers and their families, who were presumed to be interested in such details, that: 'the engines we shall use will be of the ordinary Coupled Bogie type, and we may possibly be favoured with one or more of Mr Johnson's Belpair Coupled Bogie type which now work some of the Manchester Expresses'.

For anyone making the journey who was content to remain on the Liverpool side of the Mersey, the brewery had arranged with the management of the Liverpool Overhead that travel on that wonderful electric railway on stilts should be free to brewery employees and their families that day. I had a glorious few hours travelling on the line myself in the early Fifties, noting that its squat, rather square coaches looked vaguely like brown loaves. (Among this publication's delightful collection of pictures is a painting by Roy Schofield – *A Rare Visitor* – of the Overhead rumbling across the docks, complete with a platelayer standing at the side of the track, cupping his hand around a cigarette in his attempts to light it in the stiff breeze that never stops blowing on Merseyside.)

If, on the other hand, these hardy day-trippers wanted to savour the seaside (more accurately, the riverside) delights of New Brighton, the first ferry boat of the day would deposit them on the Wirral shore at about 8.15. Since the special trains didn't start leaving Liverpool Central for the journey home until 8pm, the excursionists were assured of a long day, provided they could stand the pace.

For those who really couldn't get enough of a good thing, it was actually possible to take the paddle-steamer *Sovereign Queen* from the Prince's Landing Stage in Liverpool and snatch a couple of hours on the Isle of Man (one of the island's little trains is also depicted in this book).

The last of the seventeen specials ('All persons *must* travel both ways by their own train', said the booklet sternly) returned its bleary-eyed cargo to Burton-on-Trent at 1.40 on Saturday morning. Except for those who had made the additional trip across to Douglas, the entire journey, including the crossing on the New Brighton ferry, had been, so to speak, on the house.

It was the sort of operation which at that date would have been unthinkable without the existence of railways. As a matter of fact it seems practically unthinkable even *with* trains. Apart from whatever it must have cost, how did they actually manage it?

Only those of us who were evacuated from the big cities as schoolchildren during World War II, or who are old enough to have endured the rigours of being shifted about in troop trains, can have experienced movement by rail on anything remotely approaching the biblical scale of the Burton Brewery Binge. I am of precisely the age to have been in time for both events and, had I been of a different temperament, I might have been put off trains for ever by these two indignities. But the railway, luckily, was in my genes. My father and my grandfather and numerous uncles were all what were then referred to (and, indeed, that's how they thought of themselves) as 'railway servants' – just clerks, you understand, bowlered or trilbied to a man, and not a shiny-topped engine-driver's cap among them, I regret to say. It was enough, though. Grandpa, a short, immensely stout gentleman with an equator where his waist should have been, had already retired by the time I was old enough to remember him. But father, as staid and as cautious as grandpa was eccentric and irresponsible, was still a hard-working railway clerk, adding up four columns of figures at a glance and – even more impressive, to my way of thinking – qualifying for cheap or sometimes free rail travel for himself, my mother and me. I don't know how it was on the other three of the Big Four railway companies, but as far as the Southern Railway was concerned, as well as privilege-rate rail travel at more or less any time, my father was allowed seven free passes a year, five for destinations on the Southern and two 'foreign' passes, 'foreign' being an exotic way of referring to the other three main line railways. Whatever else lack of money prevented us from doing, we didn't go short of train journeys.

Predatory boarding-house landladies had been a notorious by-product of the sea-bathing cult as far back as the late eighteenth century. They were the subject of so many jokes (true words spoken in jest all too often) right through the last century and well on into this one, that it is possible to get the impression that, apart from the minority of holidaymakers who could afford hotels, everybody who took a holiday by the sea lodged in private houses that were only minimally adapted to accommodate them. But there was another way of doing it, known as Staying With Relations. The Victorians and Edwardians went in for enormous families, enough of whose members survived infancy to ensure a generous supply of people with whom one could claim some kind of kinship, no matter how tenuous. Often these uncles and aunts and cousins

'Smile Please' (see p. 79)
George Busby, GRA

many times removed had settled in places worth visiting for a holiday. For their part a little extra cash was always welcome, so, to their mutual benefit, it became the custom for loosely connected units of far-flung families to tolerate each other for a week or a fortnight each year.

We were lucky. Aunt Annie and Uncle Gordon lived in Cornwall, occupying one of a row of one-time tin-mine cottages in the middle of a Sahara of sandhills high above Perranporth. Never was a 'foreign' pass better named than the one which carried me, fit to explode with suppressed excitement, to that mysterious county where tiny hamlets had names like Goonbell; where rudimentary little halts had resounding titles: 'Trewerry and Trerice'; and where the conical spoil tips of the china-clay workings in distant mid-Cornwall ('if you can see the clay tips, it's going to rain') looked like the landscape of another planet in some other galaxy.

I feel rather sorry for anyone who has never enjoyed the intricate delights of regularly travelling by train to reach a holiday destination. I don't mean the brief, impersonal dash from Victoria to Gatwick, or that strange scamper in and out of the London Transport rabbit warren by Piccadilly Line to Heathrow, journeys which are frequently only short preludes to long residences in airport lounges. I'm talking of holidays, or even days out, when the train was the one thing that made the event possible.

At this point we must beware of nostalgia. Many people looking through this beautiful book and deriving, I hope, intense pleasure from it, are liable nonetheless to accuse the artists and me, the author of this extended caption to their work, of wallowing in nostalgia. I prefer to think of what we are presenting as the record of recent social history in a personal and, above all, affectionate way. It is not completely steeped in

Windows on the Past (see p. 79)
Norman Elford, GRA

the past in any case. For instance, if by some mischance you have never been in a train among children, either as one of them yourself, as a parent, or simply as another passenger hoping that they will be getting off before you do, let me assure you of the absolute verity of David Charlesworth's painting, *Children's Corner*. Although the rolling-stock is quite old – the high-backed seat, almost like a settle, is evidence of that – the occasion the work depicts is a relatively recent one as you can tell by the circular 'No Smoking' transfer on the window as opposed to the earlier triangular style. The way the three children are dressed is also of the Eighties. Otherwise the picture is nearly timeless. For as long as there have been, and will be, visits for children to the seaside, and trains to take them there, and coloured fizz in bottles and straws to drink it through, and potato crisps and books and drawing-pads to keep the kids quiet, please God, on the way, there have been and will be scenes like that.

By the same token, I believe that if I presume to set down my own memories and observations about going to the seaside by train, while the details may differ from other people's, there will be enough of common experience in them to make them at least recognisable to a wide range of readers.

The holiday, like Christmas and one's own birthday, was an annual event. Everybody knows that to any child up to the age of ten or twelve, a year is roughly the equivalent of a geological period. This conception of time is somehow conveyed by Laurence Roche's painting *Until Next*

Year, with its foreground of empty railway tracks and practically deserted beach, and the distant pier, no doubt similarly uninhabited, silhouetted against the sky. The immense gap, therefore, between one holiday and the next meant that you could never become blasé about going away. Furthermore, the sheer rarity of the occasion made it imperative not only to extract every last ounce of pleasure from the fortnight itself, but to extend what you might call its catchment area as far as possible into the weeks both before and after the event.

For me the first sparks of excitement were struck by the arrival of the letter with the Perranporth postmark that confirmed, in Aunt Annie's untidy handwriting, that it was all right for us to come as usual. Then began the packing.

In our family, packing was no last-minute flinging together of bare essentials. Not for us the comic-strip convention of the bulging suitcase with the stray sock trailing out from under the scarcely closable lid. Dad, as a good railwayman, believed in PLA – Passengers' Luggage in Advance – and our luggage somehow managed to fill an entire trunk. I often wonder now what on earth we needed that it should have assumed such bulk. But again the answer lies in the fact that so many changes have occurred within the span of a single lifetime. In the days of which I'm writing the coin-op laundry and the tumble-dryer were still many years in the future. So were quick-drying fabrics and therefore you had to take enough clobber with you to see you through the whole two weeks. Even swimming costumes were made of wool, which was not too bad going into the water but sheer hell coming out, since by then the garment had absorbed so much water and trawled up so much sand that both it and the wearer tended to sag under the unprecedented weight. It was therefore wise to have a spare dry costume to put on while the wet one was spread out to dry on the rocks.

But I'm getting ahead of myself. The packing was a slow process and its logistics were complex. You couldn't wear *this* today because it had to go in the trunk; or you'd better not wear *that* for there would never be time to get it washed and dried before it had to be packed. And it all had to be ready by a certain day for the van to come and collect. That was another moment of great significance, a sign that we really were going and that it wasn't all a delirious dream brought on by the sun which seemed to shine perpetually during those mid-Thirties summers. Precisely how far in advance the trunk went I can't remember, nor do I ever recall giving much thought to how it was conveyed. Looking back, I suppose it must have travelled in some four-wheeled, loose-coupled luggage van, or perhaps even a succession of them, shunted in and out of marshalling yards and sidings across the breadth of southern England. I certainly don't remember it ever failing to get there before we did.

Then came the actual journey. It began prosaically enough by suburban Southern electric. That was a fairly routine experience for me, but I enjoyed any ride in any train, and, like many another small boy, I tried to imitate accurately the sounds which accompanied it. The slightly abrasive hum of the motors and the curious mumbling of the brake pumps were easy enough, but it was impossible to reproduce vocally the jingling, as of a horse's harness, which I suppose must have come from the loosely suspended metal shoes which picked up the current from the third rail.

After that there was a short trip on the Bakerloo Line where the close confines of the tunnel scrambled all the sounds into one continuous rumbling roar of indeterminate pitch. Finally came the climb up the broad steps that led from the Tube to the very concourse – dad taught me early on that for some reason it was known as The Lawn – of Paddington Station.

Everything else – the letter-writing, the packing, the planning, the sandwich-cutting, the flask-filling, the purchase by my father of a handsome booklet called *Through the Window* which described in detail the whole course of the line from Paddington to Penzance (where is it now? what would it be worth?) – had all been in preparation for this moment. This is where the holiday really began.

It imposed a considerable strain on my loyalties, of course. Father was a Southern man and had been a London, Brighton and South Coast man before that (he first went to work at the age of 13½, wearing a bowler hat which, as he put it, 'nearly sliced the top of my head off like a boiled egg'). I dutifully loved the Southern's dark green electrics and the 'Lord Nelsons' and the Schools Class engines and the little push-pull train that panted along the tiny branch line from Dunton Green to Westerham. But at holiday time I was ready to admit that Great Western locomotives were the most beautiful in the world. There was something dainty about even the biggest of them, while the smallest, especially the Prairie tanks behind which we would finish our journey (one is depicted in A. L. Hammonds' *Arrival at St Ives*), were downright pretty.

The journey was a long one in those days, but not for as much as an inch was it boring. The dreary plain on the western edge of London was already ugly in a half-hearted way, never quite deciding whether to be industrial or residential. Even so, on top of a plethora of unfamiliar trains which were good to see, there were other things to look out for. At Hayes was the HMV record factory where, in the most famous trade mark in the world, Nipper the dog cocked his ear at the horn of a very early wind-up gramophone. Next to trains and trams and buses I loved gramophone

records – of almost any kind of music, for they were desirable objects in their own right. It was from record labels that I first learned to read, and later on in life I actually worked in the record industry, though not for HMV.

On the other side of the line, at Southall, AEC built the engines and chassis of London buses, and you could often see the skeletal beginnings of what might one day become our local no 12s or 194s or 108s (*they* ran through Blackwall Tunnel, another minor adventure).

The next chapter of the annual story began as soon as the train was clear of Reading. Once into the real Berkshire countryside nothing remained to remind you of London. Some of my future lay in those parts, but how was I to know, as I gazed from my corner seat while Newbury went by, that in a few years' time I would be back, together with a squad of other reluctant conscripts, trying to keep an absurd forage cap on my head, stamping my booted feet in mechanical response to the orders of one Flight-Sergeant Paterson as he tried to teach us the choreography of square-bashing on Greenham Common? The ripe counties of south-west England rolled steadily by, missing only Dorset where, much later still, I was to discover another version of Paradise.

It's a wonder I have any proper nose left at all, so continuously did I keep it pressed against the carriage window, especially on those long inclines which became increasingly noticeable as the train headed westwards. For a steam locomotive a long bank was hard work. It was harder

Looe – Summer Sunday (see p. 79)
Stephen Warnes

work still for the fireman, a now almost vanished craftsman who was expected to use both brawn and brain for considerable periods at a time and who was taken utterly for granted by most of what British Rail now calls its 'customers'. As he swung his shovel, shifting a ton or two of boulder-like coal while we munched our sandwiches and sipped tea from the ingenious hollow caps of Thermos flasks, the engine would slog uphill with its huge load, sometimes slowing to a pace that made you feel you could jump out and run alongside it. One such climb and its compensating rush down the other side separated Somerset and Devon. Entry into Devon was an important moment for a couple of reasons. One was that we had now come a long way, and that alone was in some mystic sense a good thing. The other was that one of the two most spectacular stretches of line on the whole journey was not far ahead.

Whatever else happened, it was essential to be on the left-hand – port – side of the train once it had gone through Exeter. First the line would skirt the saltings on the western side of the Exe estuary, and, on a clear day, since steam engines obligingly waved aloft a ragged white standard to mark their passage, you might pick out the Southern's trains running along the shore on the other side. Then, just after Starcross, would begin one of the most photographed, painted, drawn, described, loved and – in truth – troublesome few miles of permanent way in Britain. At the foot of the red ochre sandstone cliffs of South Devon, the main line to the west relied, and still relies, on keeping a precarious foothold along the top of the sea wall. How close the trains come to getting their feet wet you can see in Philip Hawkins' painting *Some Things Never Change*. Just above the beach, a diesel-electric powered Inter-City dashes out of one of the short tunnels. On the beach itself, wearing a knotted handkerchief in place of a crown, is a present-day Canute, snoozing in a deckchair, oblivious to both train and tide. Sometimes the sea rises in wrath and claims stretches of sea wall and railway track for itself, calling for emergency action and costly repairs. Most of the time, luckily, the water knows its place, and quietly tolerates the inquisitive feet, puny nets and inefficient buckets of small children, like the ones you see at Dawlish in Peter Annable's *Summer Holidays*.

Dawlish – it sounds like a state of mind: 'I feel a bit dawlish today; let's not go very far.'

At Teignmouth would come the long, tilting curve which carried the line back inland, this time up the Teign estuary. Again, how could I have possibly guessed that in a few summers' time I would be getting off a train there as a re-evacuee. Some London schools hadn't been moved very far in 1939. Ours had descended upon Oxted at the foot of the North Downs. In 1944, thickets of barrage balloons sprouted along all the southern approaches to London in an attempt to bring down the German V-1s which burbled their pilotless and erratic way towards the capital in a desperate enemy reaction to the Allied invasion of Europe. Rational schooling became impossible, so off we went again. Thus I came to spend the last year of the war, and my final year at school, in the delectable town – half resort, half sea port – that had previously been just a blur with a name.

The next stop was Newton Abbot, not yet famous for its book publishing. And then the engine (or maybe even engines by this time) would really begin to labour as the train clambered through the South Devon hills. Everything was worth seeing, and the big windows in the corridors gave smallish persons a particularly good view. But the really deep windows appeared to be in the restaurant cars. One year father lashed out on afternoon tea and, by some miracle of timing, we were in the dining car just as the train reached the second best spectacle – Saltash Bridge. The best place to see a bridge is, of course, from practically everywhere but the bridge itself. Fortunately the alignment curves into Saltash Bridge at both ends, giving the passenger an oblique view of those great humped tubular girders – two tremendous arcs – that resemble the way the Loch Ness Monster's neck is always drawn. Then we would be on the bridge itself, and the emotive moment would have arrived of crossing from England into Cornwall. From this point the stations and halts would have names that not even the writers of fiction would have dared to invent: Menheniot, Liskeard, Par, Probus and Ladock.

We were getting near now. You could look down on most of the modest city of Truro (which once boasted Cornwall's only set of traffic lights) from the GWR's tall viaduct. Then Chacewater, a name, it seemed, without a place. But this is where you changed for Perranporth; this was the outpost from which one of those supremely elegant little tank engines would haul its two coaches along a single track branch, full of impetuous ninety-degree changes of direction and more crazy poetry – Mount Hawke Halt, St Agnes, Mithian. To get into Perranporth itself, with its island platform, neat sidings, signal box and general air of scaled-down importance, the line negotiated a remarkable hairpin cutting, which I always used to try to reproduce in mashed potato at mealtimes for weeks after.

As so often on the Great Western, the station stood aloof from the little town it was meant to serve. It was inconvenient, I suppose, but ideal for a solitary child like myself since it constituted an entirely separate place to go, as remote from my ordinary life as was Perranporth's vast beach. I would spend hours at Perranporth Station, gazing up the long aisle of the coombe the line followed on the way to its ultimate destination of Newquay. In the warm drowsy silences between trains I could dangle my legs over the edge of the stone-flagged platform and watch dragonflies, the colour of spilled oil, rise menacingly from the reed-beds in the stream at the foot of the bank. And when I had stayed too long and the unaccustomed rich local cream had had its effect and I was caught short, Mr Miners, the signalman, would come down from his box and unlock the toilet so that I didn't have to squander a penny on inessentials. To be on those terms with a big railway company, I felt, meant you were *in*.

I got to know the drivers, too; gentle Cornishmen with accents so far west as to sound practically transatlantic. Year after year they would help me up onto the footplate, where I would stand awkwardly, flinching at the fire (suddenly they were *big* engines) and longing for an engineman's shiny-crowned cap instead of the ludicrous peaked acorn cup I wore as a schoolboy. And I listened to their anecdotes, wonderful, trivial scraps about the daily life of that now vanished branch line. Among the few I remember after all this time one concerned a willing but not especially bright porter who worked on the station at St Agnes. He was seen one day to dash off the platform and along the track in pursuit of a small animal, shouting: 'Stop that dog! He's a parcel!'

It looks as though I have run past my own danger signals and, despite my comments regarding reminiscing, for several pages now have been plunging out of control into darkest Nostalgia. All this stuff about steam engines could have led you to think that you had been keeping company with yet another eccentric dweller in the past – the equivalent in railway terms of what jazz enthusiasts call a 'mouldy fig'. Once again I plead 'not guilty'. I wrote about my childhood holidays because, of all memories, those of childhood are the most vivid and usually the most accurate. Nor are they only visual. Fifty-odd years later I can *hear* the little spitting noise – the sound a human would make getting rid of an apple pip – that came from somewhere in the exquisitely designed motion of Great Western engines. If I try hard enough I can *smell* third-class upholstery, or re-create somewhere in my head the aroma given off by what I suppose must have been a mixture of hot oil and steam. I can *feel* the cinder in my eye, something I experienced far too often ever to forget either the sting

Camping Coach, Abererch, North Wales, Late 1930s (see p. 79)
Albert Lawrence Hammonds, GRA

of it, or the surprise, when it was finally removed on the corner of an adult's handkerchief, at finding that it was only a tiny speck and not something the size of a lump of coke. I can remember the rituals – heaving up the window by its genuine leather strap to keep out the sulphurous smoke when the train went into a tunnel. I also concentrated on childhood holidays rather than grown-up ones because a holiday, like Christmas, is to a child an even more intense experience than it is to an adult.

Only artists retain that childlike capacity for intensity, and they, fortunate souls, have the ability to transmit their excitement from their hearts, up to their brains, down their arms and onto the canvas or paper. Since this is primarily a book of paintings and drawings evocative of going to the seaside by train, I felt that the least I could do was to try to match the artists' fervour. And there is one aspect where the mere scribbler of words might even be able to come to the aid of his pictorial colleagues, and that is to try to explain to the sceptical the aesthetic side of a love of trains. That includes not merely the machines that achieved motion by combining the medieval elements of fire and water, but almost anything that runs on rails under its own power.

The steam engine must be our starting point, however, for it is beyond question the nearest humankind has ever come to building a mechanical contrivance which not only possesses something suspiciously like a will of its own, but also responds, as an animal might, in an individual way to individual treatment. I'm still not sure what to be when I grow up, but I certainly went through the universal boyhood phase of wanting to be an engine driver. If chance had led me in that direction instead of into more lowly pursuits like librarianship and writing and broadcasting, I think I would have enjoyed it. Assuming that I could have endured getting dirty and oily, and having the lower half of my body exposed to a furnace and the upper half to the weather, I would have gained satisfaction from the sheer subtle craftsmanship of the job.

The look of an engine would have engendered pleasure in me also. Very few steam locomotives have ever been positively ugly. Richard Trevithick's pioneering contraption of 1804 was perhaps a little quaint, a strange amalgam of a giant spinning-wheel and an old-fashioned roadmenders' tar boiler. Some of O. V. S. Bulleid's bizarre experiments on the Southern in the Forties might have given pain to the sensitive. But Trevithick, who one day must get his full due, had nothing to go on – there was simply no one before him. Bulleid was trying to discover how far he could go with the steam technology of his day. Bulleid, in any case, was accidentally responsible for some of the most beautiful engines ever to run in Britain. After other hands had taken off the casing and replaced some of Bulleid's mechanical extravagances, the *Merchant Navy* and

West Country Pacifics were handsome in the extreme. There's one in M. A. Turner's painting of Southampton, and the smokebox of another is visible in J. E. Wigston's montage entitled *Golden Days*.

Until very recent times, electric multiple units have seldom risen above the grimly functional, but some electric locomotives have had a certain distinction about them. The stylish example – now no more, alas – in M. A. Turner's *Night Ferry* at Victoria is a case in point.

Track itself is graceful: there are no corners, just *art nouveau* curves. Points and crossings which daily direct the passage of loads totalling thousands of tons have the appearance of delicate silver tracery, while single track, threading its way, for instance, through the rocks above a lochside on the West Highland line, actually enhances the loneliness, the way one small sound will intensify a silence. Visually, it's sad that semaphore signals, which, if there were enough of them on one gantry, created their own skyline, have almost disappeared. But many of the colour light signals that have replaced them are, without knowing it, very fine pieces of modern statuary.

This is no place to get involved in the polemics of rail *v* road, but every time I walk along the pavement down a street which was once quiet, with the jugger-naughty traffic clocking up about six on the Richter scale, I know that my love of trains is not a sentimental thing but a practical one. All the same, a little sentiment to end on will do no harm. It concerns two institutions, both connected with Brighton, where Dr Russell almost started the whole business off over two hundred years ago; both are represented in this book; one survives and the other has vanished. The survivor is Volk's Electric Railway, the first of its kind in Britain, which laid its narrow gauge rails along the Brighton sea-front in the late nineteenth century. It still operates ancient, excrutiatingly slow, four-wheeled cars, and it is unthinkable that one should visit Brighton without riding on it.

The other is the now extinct Brighton Belle. It was unique because it consisted of the only all-Pullman electric multiple units in the world – a wonderful oddity in an era of increasing standardisation. I never travelled in it as a child (I imagine that privilege-ticket- and pass-holders were barred from it), but I did manage to patronise it not long before its demise in 1972. I still have the tariff. The wine list includes a non-vintage champagne at £1.42 a half-bottle. There are eleven other wines in its 'cellar' and ten varieties of beer. To eat, there are grilled kippers (11p each), grilled sirloin steak with tomato, peas and chips for 95p. Tea is 9p a pot and a round of buttered toast 5½p. I'm something of a connoisseur of toast, and the Belle has got it just right. On the strength of its toast alone, the Brighton Belle deserves to be reinstated forthwith.

PETER CLAYTON

Arrival at St Ives on a Hot Summer's Day in the Early 1950s (see p. 65)
Albert Lawrence Hammonds, GRA

Famous Departure (see p. 65)
Mike Turner, GRA

Bank Holiday Roster (see p. 65)
John Harrison, GRA

Golden Days (see p. 65)
John E. Wigston, GRA

Night Ferry (see p. 65)
Mike Turner GRA

Carnforth Station (see p. 66)
John S. Gibb, GRA

Five Shilling Excursion (see p. 66)
John Harrison, GRA

The Children's Corner (see p. 66)
David Charlesworth, GRA

Holiday Express (see p. 66)
Roy Schofield, GRA

Spring Tides, the Duddon Estuary (see p. 66)
Alexander P. Harris, GRA

Return to Southsea (see p. 67)
Norman Elford, GRA

Up the Coast (see p. 67)
Peter Owen Jones, GRA

The Forth Bridge (see p. 67)
Peter Annable, GRA

Incoming Tide (see p. 68)
Stephen Warnes

Clacton Campers (see p. 68)
Malcolm Root, GRA

Little Girl Arriving at Butlins (see p. 68)
William Roberts

Across the Straits (see p. 68)
George Busby, GRA

Road to the Isles (see p. 69)
Eric Oldham

Barmouth Bridge (see p. 69)
Gerald Broom, GRA

Harwich Quay. (with licence) "End of the line." Copyright R.P.Milliken 1989.

End of the Line (see p. 69)
Rob Milliken, GRA

Before the Crowds Came (see p. 70)
George Busby, GRA

Clean Beaches, Pure Seas and Electric Trains (see p. 70)
Mike Turner, GRA

Cornish Harbour, Mevagissey in the 1980s (see p. 70)
Albert Lawrence Hammonds, GRA

A Rare Visitor (see p. 70)
Roy Schofield, GRA

The King George Dock, Hull (see p. 71)
Peter Owen Jones, GRA

Port Penrhyn (see p. 71)
George Busby, GRA

Summer in Campbeltown (see p. 71)
George Busby, GRA

Glen Wyllin Viaduct, Isle of Man (see p. 72)
Peter Annable, GRA

Allhallows-on-Sea (see p. 72)
Laurence Roche, GRA

43XX Class GWR Train Near Barmouth Junction (see p. 72)
Eric Bottomley, GRA

Evening Mellows the Big Port (see p. 72)
Mike Turner, GRA

New Zealand Bound (see p. 72)
John E. Wigston, GRA

The Industrial Seaside (Past and Present) (see p. 72)
Laurence Roche, GRA

The Seaside (Somewhere Along the Sussex Coast) (see p. 73)
Laurence Roche, GRA

Some Things Never Change (see p. 73)
Philip D. Hawkins, GRA

Summer Holidays (see p. 73)
Peter Annable, GRA

Down by the Sea (see p. 73)
Des Harradine

Ramsgate, Summer Evening (see p. 73)
George Busby, GRA

Seaside Solitude (see p. 73)
Malcolm Root, GRA

The Last Resort (see p. 73)
William Knox

All Good Things Come to an End (see p. 74)
G. Peter M. Green, GRA

Barmouth Viaduct from the Harbour in June 1987 (see p. 74)
Albert Lawrence Hammonds, GRA

The Royal Mails to London (see p. 74)
John E. Wigston, GRA

Harwich – Train Ferry Terminal (see p. 74)
Rob Milliken, GRA

Evening Departure (see p. 74)
Peter Owen Jones, GRA

**DMU Leaving Barmouth Station for Machynlleth on a
Summer's Afternoon in 1988** (see p. 76)
Albert Lawrence Hammonds, GRA

Home from the Seaside (see p. 76)
Philip D. Hawkins, GRA

Until Next Year (see p. 76)
Laurence Roche, GRA

THE COLOUR PLATES

The Colour Plates: Extended Descriptions

Sizes quoted are approximate and include mounts but not frames.

Arrival at St Ives on a Hot Summer's Day in the Early 1950s
Albert Lawrence Hammonds, GRA
Oils, 28 × 36 in (71 × 91 cm)

The scene depicts the complete Cornish Riviera Express, with its ten coaches terminating at St Ives behind a 4500 class 2–6–2T in August 1953. The railway was so close to the beach that you could virtually step off the train and straight on to the sands. At this period most people travelled to the seaside by train, and carriages and station platforms were always crowded with eager holidaymakers. Weatherwise, the artist has tried to capture the ideal summer's day with clear blue sky, crystal sea and golden sands on which crowds of people are soaking up the sun.

Famous Departure
Mike Turner, GRA
Gouache, 15 × 20 in (38 × 50 cm)

It is 1967 and already the new uniforms worn by staff at Victoria Station reflect the new British Rail corporate image. The Brighton Belle, however, is still majestic in its Pullman livery that provided a standard of excellence which was unsurpassed for many years.

The 'electric' Belle was introduced on 1 January 1933 to replace the old steam service once electrification between London and Brighton was complete. The units themselves were unique as they provided the only motor-propelled Pullman cars ever built.

The Brighton Belle saw its last days painted in the then standard BR blue and grey livery. It was finally withdrawn on 30 April 1972.

Bank Holiday Roster
John Harrison, GRA
Inks, 21 × 25 in (53 × 63 cm)

The engine arrangements board was familiar, in some shape or size, to every footplate man. Hand written by the foreman or clerk, they were often works of art in their own right. This painting is loosely based on the Newton Heath board, reputed to have been one of the largest in Britain. It shows the Manchester excursions to the seaside and the engine allotted to each duty. Bank holiday workings often stretched a shed's allocation of locomotives to its limits and brought forth some choice remarks when drivers and firemen booked on and saw which engine they were expected to cope with.

Golden Days
John E. Wigston, GRA
Watercolour, 28 × 20 in (71 × 51 cm)

Little did the artist realise all those years ago when he stood, during his loco-spotting days, admiring those wonderful railway posters, that they would form a backdrop to one of his own works that depicted those 'golden days' of travelling to the seaside by a civilised mode of transport.

The artist hopes that the montage does justice to those artists, among them Jack Merritt, Harry Riley and Paul B. Mann, who painted many of these posters. His intention was to re-create that bubble of excitement he felt as a young lad when he was about to travel on the railways, with his parents or brother, or was off and away for two weeks with the scouts – golden days!

Night Ferry
Mike Turner GRA
Gouache, 17 × 22 in (43 × 56 cm)

Victoria Station, London, is synonymous with the South Coast and this scene in 1964 echoes to the sounds of electric trains clattering over a maze of track and points.

The night ferry is preparing to depart with its continental coaches, denoting a period when overnight travel from London to Paris reflected a charm of its own in a relaxed and composed environment.

Alas, the train is no more, but the future promises a new era with the introduction of 'Eurocity rail travel'.

Southsea Miniature Railway (see p. 79)
Norman Elford, GRA

Carnforth Station
John S. Gibb, GRA
Pencil, 26 × 36 in (66 × 91 cm)

It is a day in late summer, 1906; the time is 3.28pm. The Furness Railway train in the station is the 3.15 arrival stopping train from Barrow-in-Furness. The children admiring the locomotive have enjoyed a day on the beach at Grange over Sands, but are now on their way home in the late afternoon – the weather, perhaps, could have been better.

Carnforth, the southern terminus of the Furness Railway, was a busy junction in pre-grouping days. It linked the FR not only with the L&NWR, whose north-south main line can be seen to the right, but also the Midland Railway. Passengers travelling from areas served by these two larger companies were able, by means of through bookings, to visit seaside resorts on the Lancashire and Cumberland coasts served by the Furness Railway.

No 36, the locomotive in charge of the 'stopper', was one of the six 4-4-0 passenger engines that were ordered in 1896 by the Furness Railway Company from Sharp Stewart & Co of Manchester.

On the L&NWR up main line, an 0-6-2 coal tank is taking advantage of a lull in south-bound passenger traffic to hurry goods vehicles through the station to the marshalling yard that was located on the south-western side of the passenger station.

All too soon, the 3.31 L&NWR stopping train to Tebay will arrive to transport the young holidaymakers back home and their day out will be just a memory.

Ice-cream and Candy Floss (see p. 79)
Malcolm Root, GRA

Five Shilling Excursion
John Harrison, GRA
Pen and wash, 21 × 26 in (53 × 66 cm)

Memories of childhood and the Lancashire landscape of bygone years – granite sets, gas lamps, steam trains and the LMS five-shilling day trips to the seaside – all is now lost in the mists of time, overtaken by asphalt, electricity, the internal combustion engine, and decimal currency.

The steam locomotive crossing the bridge is a relic of an even earlier period: one of the Lancashire and Yorkshire Railway's ubiquitous 2-4-2 radial tanks. Designed by John A. F. Aspinall and built in considerable numbers at Horwich Locomotive Works, they were seen all over the L&Y system on most types of traffic.

The Children's Corner
David Charlesworth, GRA
Oils, 12 × 16 in (30 × 41 cm)

Three young friends make their own homely corner in an open Mk 1. Whatever the destination, any long railway journey will find adults and children alike surrounding themselves with the clutter of travel – magazines, books, toys, crisp packets and 'pop'.

The initial euphoria of the train has passed and the children become listless and tired. Excitement again stirs when the sea suddenly comes into view on the distant horizon. Eager anticipation is reawakened, and thoughts again turn to the bucket, spade and candy floss.

Holiday Express
Roy Schofield, GRA
Gouache, 13 × 16½ in (33 × 42 cm)

A memorable newspaper heading defines the date of this scene as 7 May 1954. Nearly six years had elapsed since the nationalisation of British Railways, but little had changed inside this ex-LMS 3rd-class side corridor coach. The generous seats and folding armrests were a style introduced by the LMS in 1932 and they became a standard feature for 3rd-class travellers on all main line systems in the UK.

At holiday times special excursion trains were designated to cope with the rush to the seaside and often comprised a rich mixture of vintage carriages. For many families, and in particular the younger members, a seaside excursion was the only opportunity they had to travel by train and the experience was very much a part of the holiday.

Spring Tides, the Duddon Estuary
Alexander P. Harris, GRA
Acrylic, 17 × 24 in (43 × 61 cm)

Fresh snow blankets the backdrop of the Coniston Fells and spring tides cover low-lying grazing alongside the Duddon estuary as a mineral train meanders southwards towards Kirkby-in-Furness on the Cumbrian coast-line.

Despite its proximity to that centre of British tourism, the Lake District, the coast and its attendant railway, with the possible exceptions of Grange over Sands and Ravenglass, are sadly overlooked by holidaymakers intent on contributing to the traffic congestion of Bowness and Keswick.

Regularly threatened with closure (especially the northern section of the line) the line's survival is assured in part by the nuclear industry at Sellafield and its attendant need for a publicly acceptable means of waste transport – ie rail. Such is 'progress'.

Return to Southsea
Norman Elford, GRA
Acrylic, 16½ × 20 in (42 × 51 cm)

This scene is familair to the artist and to many thousands of visitors to the Isle of Wight – a scene, alas, no longer with us, as the British Rail Sealink ferries which once operated the Portsmouth to Ryde route have now been replaced by faster, more efficient catamarans – but sadly missed is the stroll around open decks with the Solent breezes ruffling the hair.

MV *Southsea*, the last survivor of the three ferries, is seen approaching the entrance to Portsmouth Harbour. She operated the route from 1948 to 1986 and at the time of writing awaits a decision regarding her future.

Up the Coast
Peter Owen Jones, GRA
Oils, 22 × 30 in (56 × 76 cm)

The line that ran along the cliff top from Scarborough up to Whitby, and then continued on to Middlesborough via Staithes was, until its closure in 1965, a magnificent switchback, better noted for its scenery and viaducts than speed. In fact, the demands made upon the locomotives were such that it was not until the LNER rebuilt some of the old north-eastern 4–6–0 tank engines into 4–6–2 A6 class that the problem was solved.

The soft shale of the area is scored by deep ravines as streams pour off the uplands of the North Yorkshire Moors, and here at Sandsend the Mickleby Beck joins the North Sea. The station was right at the northern end of the viaduct, perched high on a cliff and approached up a 1 in 50 incline from almost sea level at East Row a mile to the south. Those A6s had to work hard all the way into the station.

The Forth Bridge
Peter Annable, GRA
Oils, 16 × 24 in (41 × 61 cm)

The world-famous Forth Bridge which carries the Edinburgh–Aberdeen main line across the Firth of Forth still ranks high among the engineering wonders of the world, although it was opened as far back as 1890 at a cost of £2½ million.

Each of the two main spans is 1,710ft across and the bridge is 157ft above the water with its main feature, the three great diamond-shaped towers, each rising to 360ft above water level.

Including the approach viaducts, the Forth Bridge measures 8,296ft or 1½ miles in length, and to prevent rusting, repainting is continuously in progress. As painting the bridge takes three years to complete, as soon as the job is completed, repainting starts again.

Plym Estuary (see p. 79)
George Busby, GRA

Torbay Express (see p. 79)
Philip D. Hawkins, GRA

The Great Dungeness Train Race (see p. 79)
G. Peter M. Green, GRA

Fort William (see p. 79)
Peter Owen Jones, GRA

Incoming Tide
Stephen Warnes
Acrylic, 30 × 36 in (76 × 91 cm)

Many seaside towns were literally made by the railways. During the annual Wakes Weeks, people from the industrial hinterland would pour along the lines to the coast, just as waves rush to the shore. This metaphor is explored in *Incoming Tide* which relies in places on realism and in other parts drifts towards abstraction.

The artist was inspired to create the central image of the locomotives in the sea – the starting point of the picture – when he observed waves breaking over a large dark rock. This became transposed into the shiny black of the Aspinall Lancashire and Yorkshire Railway engines.

Clacton Campers
Malcolm Root, GRA
Oils, 24 × 30 in (61 × 76 cm)

The station at Clacton-on-Sea in Essex, like many other seaside railway stations, was a hive of activity all through the summer. Many of the Butlin's campers arrived on the special summer expresses from London and immediately were taken under the wing of the famous Butlin's Redcoats and shown the buses that would take them to the nearby holiday camp. On the Butlin's run on this particular day in the late 1950s was locomotive class B17, No 61651 *Derby County*. The lucky passengers on this trip look set for a fine week.

Little Girl Arriving at Butlins
William Roberts
OIl, 24 × 48 in (61 × 122 cm)

The artist executed this painting mainly from memory. The period is around 1960, when the Cambrian coastline on a summer Saturday was packed with extra trains for the holiday camp near Pwllheli.

The station was built a few years after the war with a double track for a few miles to Afon Wen, the junction with the LMS branch line to Bangor.

The artist worked for a period at the holiday camp and had seen the delight of children when they arrived there. The station is now overgrown and derelict, but a single track still runs through to Pwllheli traversed by the occasional Sprinter.

Across the Straits
George Busby, GRA
Watercolour, 18 × 24 in (46 × 61 cm)

Low tide on a summer evening. The Britannia Bridge is a delicate line against the sky, running between the tree-lined banks of the Menai Strait.

Travellers from the mainland of North Wales to the Isle of Anglesey may now travel either by road or rail across the bridge. Originally a railway bridge of tubular structure, it was the work of Robert Stephenson and was built in 1850.

As well as providing a link for holidaymakers in Anglesey, the bridge carries the line to Holyhead where passengers may embark for the sea trip to Ireland.

Road to the Isles
Eric Oldham
Watercolour/gouache, 12 × 20 in (31 × 51 cm)

For those contemplating journeys to the sea, the Road to the Isles evokes a special kind of magic. The old Dingwall and Skye line, which was built by the Highland Railway in 1870 as far as Strome Ferry, is a traveller's joy. Mountain vistas that are mirrored in still waters alternate with deer forests, raging torrents, lochs and heather-clad slopes of intense colour.

The final stretch of the line to Kyle of Lochalsh, which was completed in 1897, is the *pièce de résistance*. Much of it blasted from the solid rock, it is one of the most remarkable coastal railways in Great Britain. Here the line twists and turns along the open shores of Loch Carron, passing through deep rock-cuttings and emerging to reveal superb views of Skye.

The painting depicts the morning train from Inverness to Kyle of Lochalsh by the shore of Loch Carron near Plockton in 1925. The locomotive is a Skye Bogie of the Highland Railway, which was built in 1882. On the formation of the London, Midlands and Scottish Railway, these engines were attired in red livery, and this mixed train is typical of the period.

Barmouth Bridge
Gerald Broom, GRA
Acrylic, 20 × 30 in (51 × 76 cm)

For most West Midlanders holidays and day-trips in post-war Britain usually meant Wales, and although the artist can remember a few sunny days at Rhyl, with an endless procession of Black 5 hauled excursions, it mostly rained. The adventures of a car-borne youth carried him further afield and he discovered Wales and its mountains. The Cader Idris was one; it terrified him, looming above Talyllyn, head in the clouds, a fearsome primeval bulk to be respected at all times.

The Cambrian line was unknown to the artist until 1985 when he enjoyed a pottering DMU ride along the coast to Barmouth and visited the location depicted with the mountain presenting its western edges in an unforgettable backdrop.

It is one thing to enthuse over a potential painting from studied photographs in the complacency of our armchairs, but how necessary and fulfilling it is to savour the subject first hand. How comfortably railways seem to blend into the landscape – another statement of nostalgia, perhaps, but even now one tends to invoke the spirit of Ruskin when a rural idyll is threatened by any modern infrastructure. Will we ever tire of the dependable ingredients that a landscape view presents? Even the clichés are essential and evergreen.

This painting, which shows a typical 1930s train hauled by a Duke and an Earl, is but a brief study of the story. The artist states that the subject matter deserves a broader traditional approach in oils, so perhaps he will be inspired again on another occasion, when in his mind's eye a little

Edwardian Beach Scene (see p. 79)
John S. Gibb, GRA

Cambrian Sharp Stewart 0-6-0 struggles out onto the Friog. . . .

The bridge surely will be replaced one day and the railway itself may go, but Cader Idris is eternal and will outlive us all.

End of the Line
Rob Milliken, GRA
Watercolour, 16 × 19 in (41 × 48 cm)

Harwich: the steady decline of the railway system at the docks meant that the train ferries died out, yet the buffer stops still stand subjected to all weather and the effects of the sea salt.

Although the artist has rearranged the scene, he has depicted certain aspects of the area around the ferry terminal as they actually are. A sea mist rolls in; all is quiet except for the sound of the bells on buoys and fog-horns. A Trinity House vessel, about to dock alongside the Trinity House Pier, is just visible through the mist.

Before the Crowds Came

George Busby, GRA
Watercolour, 18 × 24 in (46 × 61 cm)

Early morning, before the season really starts. The promenade is empty, rust stains the railings. The Volks Electric Railway looks particularly sad without its little coaches bulging with holidaymakers intent on enjoying the ride from Palace Pier to Black Rock. During the holiday season it rattles over the pebble beaches, when occasionally the waves lap beneath the track for a brief moment. Sometimes it stops at the halfway station to allow its passengers to alight and visit the noisy funfair.

Magnus Volk opened his electric railway on Brighton sea-front in 1883. It was the first railway of its kind in the world and still attracts visitors, both young and old.

Clean Beaches, Pure Seas and Electric Trains

Mike Turner, GRA
Gouache, 22 × 22 in (56 × 56 cm)

In this idealistic vision of the future in which people behave more responsibly towards their environment than they do today, beaches are clean, there is no litter and one can swim in a sea that is free from the threat of dangerous poisons and sewage lurking beneath the waves.

Electric trains, energy efficient and more ecologically sound, take a leading role in the world of transport once more. Here Network South East provides the service with its Wessex Electric units.

Cornish Harbour, Mevagissey in the 1980s

Albert Lawrence Hammonds, GRA
Oils, 28 × 36 in (71 × 91 cm)

The picture of fishing boats nestling in the shelter of a Cornish harbour on a hot summer's day immediately brings to mind the smell of the sea and happy holidays spent in the West Country. This painting depicts a scene typical of the West Country, especially of Cornwall, when visitors have arrived at the seaside.

A Rare Visitor

Roy Schofield, GRA
Mixed medium, 12½ × 17 in (32 × 43 cm)

For sixty-three years the Liverpool Overhead Railway was unique, being the only completely elevated system in the UK. Built in 1893, it survived until 1956 and somehow managed to avoid nationalisation in 1948.

The 6½-mile journey along the LOR afforded spendid views over the docks and shipping generally on the River Mersey.

During the LOR's early history Liverpool was a major port and many of the larger Atlantic liners sailed from there. The *Aquitania*, depicted here, sailed from Liverpool on her maiden voyage. When World War I began on 4 August 1914, the *Aquitania* was immediately requisitioned as an armed merchant cruiser, although she had made only three round trips (Liverpool–New York).

On returning to peace-time duties, the *Aquitania* spent the next twenty

Dawlish Departure (see p. 80)
Peter Annable, GRA

years on the Southampton–New York route. A rare visit to Liverpool occurred in August 1940 when she was converted to a troop-ship and played an important role in World War II. The *Aquitania* was the only 'four stacker' to survive both world wars virtually unscathed.

The painting depicts 'the rare visitor' in Gladstone Dock at the Seaforth end of the Liverpool Overhead Railway.

The King George Dock, Hull
Peter Owen Jones, GRA
Watercolour, 19 × 19 in (48 × 48 in)

Many docks and harbours were once privately owned while others belonged to railway companies. The King George Dock at Hull was operated by the London and North Eastern Railway which maintained a substantial fleet of tank locomotives that were capable of negotiating the tight radius curves within the complex. The dock contained mainly class J72s and J77s, with a smattering of the diminutive 0–4–0 Y8s, as seen here on the quayside, dwarfed by the ships and cranes.

Port Penrhyn
George Busby, GRA
Gouache, 18 × 24 in (46 × 61 cm)

The Penrhyn narrow gauge railway was used solely to carry slate the 6 miles down from the large quarries at Bethesda to Port Penrhyn, near Bangor. Many locomotives were employed on the actual quarry workings, but the transportation of slate down to Port Penrhyn was the province of two little locomotives named *Blanche* and *Linda*. These were built in 1893 by the Hunslet Engine Company and given the maker's numbers 589 and 590.

At the port, the narrow gauge railway ran alongside the standard gauge line. At this point the slate was trans-shipped to the trucks of the main line railway. The Penrhyn railway closed in 1963, its work having been taken over by road transport.

Summer in Campbeltown
George Busby, GRA
Watercolour, 18 × 24 in (46 × 61 cm)

The Campbeltown and Machrihanish narrow gauge railway ran the 6 miles between the eastern and western shores of the Mull of Kintyre. Originally a colliery line, it was rebuilt and extended in 1906 to cater for an increasing summer tourist trade. Visitors could disembark from the Clyde passenger steamers at Campbeltown and board the train to Machrihanish to enjoy the giant breakers of the Atlantic.

During the winter only trains from the colliery used the line. At the beginning of the 1930s tourism was no longer sufficient to support the railway and the colliery also closed. The railway ceased to operate in 1932.

Chimney – Bird (see p. 80)
Philip D. Hawkins, GRA

Punch and Judy (see p. 80)
Roy Putt

Dover Harbour (see p. 80)
G. Peter M. Green, GRA

Glen Wyllin Viaduct, Isle of Man

Peter Annable, GRA
Watercolour, 15 × 19 in (38 × 48 cm)

The viaduct, the main engineering structure on the Isle of Man, with its plate girders and stone pillars, is situated a few hundred yards from Kirk Michael Station on the Douglas to Ramsey line.

Below the viaduct the gardens in the glen were privately owned until 1935 when they were taken over by the Manx Northern Railway. The Glen Wyllin Pleasure Grounds were a popular venue for day excursions for all the family, with a boating lake, gardens and amusements.

The pathway beneath the viaduct leads to the pleasure grounds and beyond to a cove at the foot of the glen with a beautiful sandy beach.

Allhallows-on-Sea

Laurence Roche, GRA
Acrylic, 18 × 28 in (46 × 71 cm)

A person out for an early morning stroll stands on the platform as if they are awaiting the first train of the day bringing the holiday crowds. Alas, the thousands did not come as envisaged at the time when Allhallows-on-Sea was opened in 1932 and the idea of another Southend emerging from the isolated north Kentish marsh was just a dream.

In its short life Allhallows-on-Sea became to some the archetypal seaside terminus serving the short branch line from Stoke Junction Halt

on the Gravesend to Port Victoria line. It did see some traffic – mainly day-trippers and campers. The line and station closed in 1961.

The artist is indebted to Gerald Daniels and J. J. Smith for the reference material and inspiration.

43XX Class GWR Train Near Barmouth Junction

Eric Bottomley, GRA
Oils, 20 × 30 in (51 × 76 cm)

A scene on the Cambrian coast around 1947 shows a GWR 43XX class rounding the curve with her train near Barmouth Junction. Some Great Western coaches are in the brown livery of this pre-nationalisation period. Both engine and coach stock are in a rather run-down condition as the railways took time to recover during the post-war years.

Branching away from the main line to Aberystwyth at Dovey Junction, Barmouth lies on the northern section of the Cambrian coast railway taking the GWR trains on their scenic journey around Cardigan Bay and terminating at Pwllheli.

Evening Mellows the Big Port

Mike Turner, GRA
Gouache, 17 × 22 in (43 × 56 cm)

The *Queen Mary* dominates this scene of Southampton, while steam still rules on the railway.

At the end of a rather humid summer's day a train from the Midlands to Bournemouth is about to depart into the low evening sun, its crew tired and hot after an exhausting day on the foot-plate.

The grand signal gantry at the end of the platform displays a superb sense of proportion and geometry, the fine detailing of the finials on each post making an interesting finishing touch.

New Zealand Bound

John E. Wigston, GRA
Watercolour, 20 × 27½ in (51 × 70 cm)

The Burrell Road locomotives *Clyde* and *Lord Roberts* of Road Engines & Kerr (Haulage) Ltd, Glasgow, deliver a class J of the New Zealand Government Railways to Clydeside from the North British Locomotive Company Ltd where it was built.

The Finnieston 130-ton crane lifts the class J for eventual loading on a ship with sister locomotives for a journey to the southern hemisphere, representing North British engineering on both islands of New Zealand.

The Industrial Seaside (Past and Present)

Laurence Roche, GRA
Acrylic, 20½ × 32 in (52 × 81 cm)

Before the decline of the coal industry in South Wales, the King's Dock, Swansea, was an important coal exporting port. Looming large and magnificent along the quay were the mighty coal hoists – gigantic mechanical structures for loading coal on to ships.

A recent return visit by the artist revealed that the hoists had gone, leaving a trail of overgrown wasteland with a solitary rusty siding. It is a sad memorial, and perhaps symbolic of our past industrial dockland heritage – hence the inspiration for the painting.

The Seaside (Somewhere Along the Sussex Coast)
Laurence Roche, GRA
Acrylic, 24 × 36 in (61 × 91 cm)

The artist states that this painting speaks for itself – save to say that it is the seaside somewhere along the Sussex coast.

Some Things Never Change
Philip D. Hawkins, GRA
Oils, 20 × 16 in (51 × 41 cm)

British Rail's image in recent years – particularly with the introduction of imaginative and colourful liveries for its locomotives and rolling-stock – has certainly done much to brighten the railway scene in Great Britain after many years of drab uniformity. The HST 125s look very attractive in the livery depicted in this picture. The location is Dawlish in Devon and it was here during 1987 while researching a completely different painting that the artist was impressed with the way that these trains seemed to blend so well into this marvellous stretch of the old Great Western Railway line. At the same time a party of holidaymakers poured onto the beach at Coryton's Cove. One of their number was sporting the time-honoured 'knotted handkerchief' much loved by British sun-bathers of the past, and settled down in his deck-chair and fell asleep. The artist made a mental note of this absurd contrast until some two years later, when, after press-ganging his father into the role of the holidaymaker, he completed the painting seen here.

Summer Holidays
Peter Annable, GRA
Watercolour, 17 × 22½ in (43 × 57 cm)

This must have been a typical scene during the inter-war years: a beach and blue sky, sunshine and a light breeze – memories of that special moment in time. The children who are playing at the water's edge are too engrossed in what they are doing to notice the train passing along the sea wall. Trains such as *The Cornishman*, *Cornish Riviera Limited* and *Torbay Express*, which meant only one thing to excited youngsters – summer holidays – regularly travelled along the Devon coastline.

This was an age when the best way to travel to 'glorious Devon' was by the Great Western Railway.

Down by the Sea
Des Harradine
Watercolour, 22 × 28 in (56 × 71 cm)

This happy beach scene at Leigh-on-Sea, Essex, noted for its cockles and shrimps, is a few miles to the west of Southend. The first trains arrived here from London (Fenchurch Street) in 1855 under the London, Tilbury and Southend Railway. In 1934 the LMS introduced the Stanier class 4 (3 cylinder) 2–6–4T engine to replace the ageing Tilbury tanks. During the twentieth century it became the seaside Mecca for thousands of bank holiday and weekend Cockney trippers.

In this painting the artist has re-created the atmosphere of the 1930s when bowler hats, braces and brown paper carrier-bags were a common part of the scene.

Ramsgate, Summer Evening
George Busby, GRA
Watercolour, 18 × 24 in (46 × 61 cm)

At the beginning of this century holidaymakers at Ramsgate could travel the length of the promenade by tram, the open upper deck making an ideal form of transport for a summer's evening. The trams on their sea-front journey passed close by the yachts and fishing-boats moored at the sea wall.

Ramsgate, as one of the leading holiday resorts of the Kent coast, was also a fishing port and an area of ship-building. The railway link with London provided reasonably priced travel for visitors to the sea, thus accelerating the popularity of seaside holidays.

Seaside Solitude
Malcolm Root, GRA
Oils, 24 × 30 in (61 × 76 cm)

Very popular in the Fifties and Sixties, Southend's pier, the longest in the world, is shown at the end of a stormy day. A solitary figure watches a train as it makes its way from the pier head to the shore, a journey of over a mile. The unlit illuminations add to the gloominess of the scene.

These trains, with their green and cream liveries, were introduced in 1949 and were made up of three motor cars and four trailers. Sadly, the Southend Pier Railway was temporarily closed in 1978 and with it went these distinctive trains.

The Last Resort
William Knox
Ink and watercolour, 16 × 21½ in (41 × 55 cm)

This painting was inspired by the many examples of early four- or six-wheeled coaching stock that ended up as a basis or addition to typical holiday homes at various coastal locations.

When the artist was about six years old he visited such a holiday home on a dark stormy night somewhere in South Wales. Memories of the pungent smell of an ill-trimmed wick on a paraffin heater and Tilley storm lamps as illumination, and the fascination of the leather straps on the drop-lights of the carriage doors were an unforgettable experience for him.

It is interesting to note that in recent years railway preservation societies such as the Bluebell Railway in Sussex have been able to rescue rare examples of coaches for subsequent restoration to running stock that otherwise would have disappeared forever.

All Good Things Come to an End
G. Peter M. Green, GRA
Oils, 16 × 20 in (41 × 51 cm)

The trouble with holidays is that they come to an end. Packing has to be done, and how do you fit into your case all those extra clothes, souvenirs and beach balls? You have to get to the station in good time lest you miss the only train of the day. You think about the fifty weeks ahead, back to the fray; and this is the day that the sun shines for the first time in a fortnight. So it's not a good moment to try to raise a smile. And if the train is late, well . . . .

The painting depicts holidaymakers assembling to catch the Devonian at Torquay, c1960.

Barmouth Viaduct from the Harbour in June 1987
Albert Lawrence Hammonds, GRA
Oils, 28 × 36 in (71 × 91 cm)

Sea, golden sands, boats set against a backdrop of mountains, with the single railway line hugging the Welsh coastline – this to the artist is the essence of a Cambrian coast holiday. Boats have always been another of A. L. Hammonds' loves and this particular scene allowed the combination of the sea and the railway in one picture.

Approaching Dawlish (see p. 80)
Philip D. Hawkins, GRA

The Royal Mails to London
John E. Wigston, GRA
Watercolour, 19½ × 27 in (49 × 68 cm)

With the completion of its new harbour facilities at Fishguard, South Wales, the Great Western Railway managed to persuade the Cunard Steamship Company for its transatlantic liners to call there so that the Royal Mails and passengers bound for London could transfer from such famous liners as the *Mauretania* to continue and shorten their journey to London by several hours.

The painting depicts the GWR tenders *Smeaton* and *Sir Francis Drake* transferring mail and passengers from the *Mauretania* to the new Harbour Station at Fishguard.

Harwich – Train Ferry Terminal
Rob Milliken, GRA
Watercolour, 21 × 27 in (53 × 68 cm)

The gantry, which dates from World War I, was originally situated at Southampton, but was moved to Harwich in 1924 when the first public Anglo-Continental train ferry service commenced. A freight traffic only service was operated by the Great Eastern Train Ferries. However, this was liquidated in 1932 and the assets were bought by the LNER. The service was suspended during the war years but after the war it was reinstated and then ran continuously until the late 1980s. The initial vessels all saw government service during the war. No 1 became HMS *Princess*, No 2 became HMS *Daffodil* and was sunk by a mine in 1945, and No 3 was lost on government service. The *Suffolk, Norfolk, Essex* and *Camb* – all ferries – were built between 1947 and 1963. The last ferry to operate was the Speedlink *Vanguard*.

The painting shows the unloading of the *Suffolk*. The artist spent much of his boyhood at the terminal, as his father worked in the engine-room of the *Suffolk*. Much time was also spent with his father watching the shunting operations at the dockside.

Evening Departure
Peter Owen Jones, GRA
Oils, 20 × 30 in (51 × 76 cm)

Family holidays in North Wales in the 1950s were a memorable experience for the enthusiastic young artist. The Jones family went in one direction and the fourteen-year-old Peter went in the other, with a camera called a Purma Special and a 7s 6d runabout ticket which gave one week's unlimited travel between Rhyl and Holyhead. These were the halcyon days of the Welch Dragon, a 2-6-2T push-and-pull service that could hurtle backwards at 60mph (96kph), and of those Holyhead Scots – the well-groomed pride of 7C. *The Old Contemptibles* was a particular favourite of the artist, probably because of its impressive name-plate, but all the Scots were magnificent engines. The artist recalls how one would restart a heavy train, which would then steadily accelerate with a rhythmic beat as it pulled away into the night.

We're Off (see p. 80)
John Harrison, GRA

Standing Room Only (see p. 80)
Roy Putt

Going Places (see p. 80)
John Hughes

DMU Leaving Barmouth Station for Machynlleth on a Summer's Afternoon in 1988
Albert Lawrence Hammonds, GRA
Oils, 28 × 36 in (17 × 91 cm)

This view of Barmouth, from the cliff-top above the town, expresses the astmosphere of the seaside. The DMU slowly wends its way over the viaduct built between rows of slate-grey boarding-houses and cafés and overlooking the small harbour full of boats. The beautiful sands and sea can be seen in the background.

As a child the artist spent all his summer holidays on the Welsh coast and to travel by train was always a treat. Having travelled up from Ruabon along the picturesque Dee estuary, his first glimpse of the sea was at Barmouth.

Home from the Seaside
Philip D. Hawkins, GRA
Oils, 20 × 30 in (51 × 76 cm)

With Birmingham Snow Hill, Wolverhampton and journey's end just a short distance away, *The Cornishman*, having left Penzance at 10.30am, climbs away from Stratford-upon-Avon along the North Warwickshire line. It approaches Danzey headed by a Stafford Road-based Castle class 4–6–0, No 5063 *Earl Baldwin*. The period is *c*1960 and, more often than not, the artist would be further along the line perched on his bicycle saddle, propped against Tyseley Bridge. He would be glancing at his watch and impatient for 6.30pm to arrive when this magnificent spectacle would come into view, if it was running to time – although at this stage of its journey it was usually behind schedule. This ritual was repeated countless times, particularly on summer evenings, until 1962 when *The Cornishman* was rerouted via the ex-Midland Railway route through Cheltenham and into Birmingham New Street.

Until Next Year
Laurence Roche, GRA
Acrylic, 21 × 27 in (53 × 68 cm)

The sun has almost set, a few people are still strolling on the beach and a boat slowly sails towards the shore. The last train of the day has gone, taking home day-trippers and contented holidaymakers after an idyllic time by the seaside. That is how we like to remember it all – until next year.

Eastbourne's Seaside Pier (see p. 80)
Albert Lawrence Hammonds, GRA

MONOCHROME WORKS OF ART

Extended Descriptions

The extended captions for these works of art are listed in order as they appear.

Measurements are given at approximate picture size.

Wakes Week Arrival (Front endpaper)
John Harrison, GRA
Pen drawing, 14½ × 21 in (37 × 53 cm)

Blackpool Central Station in the Thirties saw the weekly arrival of thousands of holidaymakers throughout the summer as each of the Lancashire mill towns had its annual Wakes Week holidays. In those halcyon days, before the birth of holidays on the Costa Brava, Central Station needed all its fourteen platforms (plus another fifteen at Blackpool North) to handle regular and excursion traffic. Now, alas, the whole station is closed and rail traffic is handled at Blackpool North, with a branch line service from Kirkham to Blackpool South on the truncated line to Central.

The Thirties-style clothes may seem excessive to our eyes, but all are authentic. The artist used his own family album of snapshots taken in Redbank Road, Bispham, as a source of reference.

Late Arrivals (Back endpaper)
Mrs M. Stella Murray-Whatley, GRA
Conte pencil, 19 × 16 in (48 × 41 cm)

The scene of this painting is Blue Anchor on the West Somerset Railway. Opened in 1862, the railway provided a new cheap and rapid means of reaching the West Somerset coast and Exmoor for a new and modest class of holidaymaker, including day-trippers. At the turn of the century the railway offered Race-Day Returns on special trains for the six race meetings held on Minehead beach and these events drew crowds of both residents and holidaymakers. Before the opening of the line, people seeking a select watering place for summer residence took the stage-coach from Washford to Minehead, Porlock and Lynmouth. Tourist travel was complemented along the seaside line at little resorts such as Blue Anchor and Dunster, by steamer trips around the Bristol Channel and into Cleeve Bay. A contemporary quote from the *West Somerset Free Press* commented of the area: 'Some capital places for bathing, the air is salubrious and bracing and the views extensive and picturesque.' The line was closed by British Railways in 1971 and reopened under private ownership in 1979.

A Warrior's Return (facing title page)
John E. Wigston, GRA
Pencil, 11 × 15½ in (28 × 39 cm)

After eight years of restoration at Hartlepool, HMS *Warrior*, the first iron battleship, is towed by the tug *Formidable* of the Alexander Towing Company to its specially built jetty opposite Portsmouth Harbour Station.

Royal Albert Bridge, Saltash (contents page)
G. Peter M. Green, GRA
Pencil, 10 × 15 in (25 × 38 cm)

As though the rail journey westward through Devon was not exciting enough for the artist, the entry into Cornwall, across Brunel's magnificent bridge over the Tamar, is perhaps the biggest thrill of all.

Norfolk Ferry Departure (acknowledgements page)
Rob Milliken, GRA
Pen and ink, 13 × 16 in (33 × 41 cm)

The *Norfolk Ferry*, built in 1951 and some 400ft long, departs from the Harwich train ferry terminal en route for Zeebrugge.

The Devonian (p. 9)
Philip D. Hawkins, GRA
Pencil, 6 × 6 in (15 × 15 cm)

Jubilee class 4-6-0, No 45651 *Shovell*, was a regular performer on the Devonian during the late Fifties and early Sixties. The train ran between Bradford and Paignton, providing a popular service particularly for holidaymakers. It ceased to run in 1975.

Edwardian Heatwave (p. 10)
Roy Putt
Pencil and watercolour, 9 × 13 in (23 × 33 cm)

A hot summer afternoon on Bournemouth beach in Edwardian days: everyone remains fully clothed and no one appears to be enjoying the benefits of sea bathing despite the available bathing machines. In the distance stands Bournemouth pier. Opened in 1880, the pier was a busy departure point for various paddle-steamers which sailed daily to other South Coast towns.

At first, Bournemouth was considered primarily as a health resort. The number of visitors increased rapidly with the coming of the railways in the

1870s. The town was served by two principal railway stations – Bournemouth Central on the LSWR line from Waterloo and Bournemouth West, the terminus of the Somerset and Dorset Joint Railway which ran from Bath.

'Smile Please' (p. 11)
George Busby, GRA
Ink, 6 × 9 in (15 × 23 cm)

'Smile please!' – the holiday photograph captures a special moment. Children pose with Charley the boatman and in the distance an engine whistle sounds.

Windows on the Past (p. 12)
Norman Elford, GRA
Pencil, 5½ × 8 in (14 × 20 cm)

Station staff confer, a passenger waits patiently for the homeward train and the graceful form of HMS *Warrior* makes a mosaic-like backdrop when seen through the windows of Portsmouth Harbour station.

Looe – Summer Sunday (p. 13)
Stephen Warnes
Pen and ink, 6½ × 8 in (16 × 20 cm)

A summer Sunday in the mid-Sixties and diesels have replaced steam on the Great Western branch lines. The depiction is of a train from Liskeard arriving at Looe Station.

Camping Coach, Abererch, North Wales, Late 1930s (p. 15)
Albert Lawrence Hammonds, GRA
Ink, 9½ × 20½ in (24 × 52 cm)

Before the war, this was a typical scene along the Cambrian coast. Every little wayside station with a siding had its camping coach. Because of their proximity to the sea and beaches, camping coaches made ideal holiday homes. During the Thirties and Forties the artist spent all his holidays at Pwllheli and he adds that it was always a treat to walk around the harbour to Abererch with its unspoilt stretch of golden sands. The days were always hot and sunny – so hot, in fact, that the sand burnt your feet when you walked on it.

Southsea Miniature Railway (p. 65)
Norman Elford, GRA
Ink, 6 × 9 in (15 × 23 cm)

The timeless appeal of the miniature steam railway is a magnet for young and old alike. Southsea's line captures the attention of strollers as a P&O ferry slips by unnoticed.

Ice-cream and Candy Floss (p. 66)
Malcolm Root, GRA
Pencil, 8½ × 5 in (21 × 13 cm)

Knowing that you won't be told off when you have candy floss all over your face and ice-cream all down your clothes, is part of the fun of a day at the seaside.

Plym Estuary (p. 67)
George Busby, GRA
Ink, 6 × 9 in (15 × 23 cm)

Threading its way along the shores of the Plym estuary, a train loaded with china clay puffs its way towards the wharf and the waiting ships.

Torbay Express (p. 67)
Philip D. Hawkins, GRA
Pencil, 6 × 6 in (15 × 15 cm)

A Castle class 4-6-0 preparing to leave Paddington during the Fifties with the *Torbay Express* to Kingswear, Devon. At this time the chocolate-and-cream livery was being restored on the Western Region Express services, reviving much of the glamour of Great Western Railway days.

The Great Dungeness Train Race (p. 68)
G. Peter M. Green, GRA
Black and white gouache, 8 × 11½ in (20 × 29 cm)

When this artist was young, a trip to the seaside would not have been complete without a ride on one of the numerous miniature railways which could be found at most seaside resorts, such as Scarborough, Southport, Blackpool and Rhyl. But undoubtedly the most exciting of all was in Kent, where the 15in gauge Romney Hythe and Dymchurch Railway runs for 14 miles (22.5km) along the coast (although, sadly, barely in sight of the sea). They have beautifully kept little engines there, and run a 'main line service'. At the Dungeness lighthouse end (shown in this depiction) there was a chance to race the train as it set off to return to Romney – always supposing, of course, that you were not lucky enough to be a passenger.

Fort William (p. 68)
Peter Owen Jones, GRA
Pen and wash, 7½ × 9½ in (19 × 24 cm)

Fort William, at the head of Loch Linnhe and the western end of the Caledonian Canal, proved an appropriate setting for the 1930s rendezvous of a Gresley K2 and the paddle-steamer *Gondolier*.

Edwardian Beach Scene (p. 69)
John S. Gibb, GRA
Pencil, 10 × 6½ in (25 × 16 cm)

A scene at the turn of the century at a seaside resort in north-west England.

Dawlish Departure (p. 70)
Peter Annable, GRA
Pencil, 8½ × 17 in (21 × 43 cm)

Lying on the South Devon coast, the family resort of Dawlish has changed little over the years with its shops set well back around a long central park through which a stream cascades under ornamental bridges down to the sea.

The railway still dominates the sea-front. This view from the park shows a west-bound train headed by a class 50 diesel locomotive pulling away from the station.

Chimney – Bird (p. 71)
Philip D. Hawkins, GRA
Pencil, 5 × 5 in (13 × 13 cm)

Steam locomotive chimneys, even rusty ones, tended to be graceful objects with beautiful flowing lines, while retaining a functional quality. Much the same could be said of the seagull. The combination is intriguing.

Punch and Judy (p. 71)
Roy Putt
Pencil, 9½ × 7 in (24 × 18 cm)

Summer 1898: a group of people begin to gather to watch the popular seaside amusement, a Punch and Judy show. Originally imported from Italy as Punchinello, Punch soon delighted Victorian audiences with his outrageous behaviour.

Dover Harbour (p. 72)
G. Peter M. Green, GRA
Black and white gouache, 10 × 13½ in (25 × 34 cm)

Dover is one of the many ports around our island where it is possible (sometimes) to walk straight from your train and onto a boat. Here the locomotive which has brought in the early morning boat train during the 1930s is seen on the harbour wall of Dover Marine Station, with the ferry from France approaching the quay-side.

Approaching Dawlish (p. 74)
Philip D. Hawkins, GRA
Pencil, 6 × 6 in (15 × 15 cm)

The view from Langstone Rock, Dawlish Warren, with a Western diesel running along the spectacular Devon coastline hauling a Paddington to West of England express during the early 1970s.

We're Off (p. 75)
John Harrison, GRA
Pen and ink, 10 × 15 in (25 × 38 cm)

The artist has recaptured that magical moment from childhood when the long wait is over: the driver leans out of his cab, the guard waves his flag and . . . we're off to the seaside!

Standing Room Only (p. 76)
Roy Putt
Gouache, 8 × 10 in (20 × 25 cm)

Holidaymakers crowd around the bandstand in early June 1896. Some find the weather mild, while others, no doubt at the seaside for health reasons, retain their top-coats.

The band's performance has attracted a large crowd, so much so that there is standing room only, all the seats having been taken. A local girl hurries past the gathering, too busy with everyday tasks to enjoy the music.

Going Places (p. 76)
John Hughes
Pen and ink, 7 × 11½ in (18 × 29 cm)

An imaginary scene in a quiet corner of Old Oak Common engine-shed: the locomotive headboards are waiting to wing their way to coastal destinations.

Transporting millions of people over many years to their seaside holidays, these named trains became institutions in their own right, epitomising leisure travel in the days when, for ordinary people, such journeys usually meant their one or two weeks' annual break.

The company's publicity department would work hard to promote these services and successfully created an atmosphere of mystique and excitement which captured the public's imagination.

These trains came into disuse when the entrepreneur was displaced by the accountant.

Eastbourne's Seaside Pier (p. 77)
Albert Lawrence Hammonds, GRA
Conte crayon, 21 × 30 in (53 × 76 cm)

The seaside pier and the cry of seagulls have epitomised summer holidays at the seaside since Victorian times.